FOSSILS AND PALEONTOLOGY FOR KIDS
Facts, Photos and Fun
Children's Fossil Books

SPEEDY
PUBLISHING

Speedy Publishing LLC
40 E. Main St. #1156
Newark, DE 19711
www.speedypublishing.com

Copyright 2015

Fossils are really interesting things, and we can learn so much from them.

The facts we
know about
organisms that
lived millions
of years ago
are found
in fossils.

Fossils are the preserved remains or traces of animals, plants, and other organisms from the remote past.

The word
fossil comes
from the Latin
word fossilis,
which means,
"dug up".

Fossils of
animals, plants
or protists
occur in
sedimentary
rock.

Fossils are
usually found
within rocks
of the Earth's
crust.

The best
ways for an
organism to
become a
fossil is if it is
buried alive or
is buried soon
after dying.

Some fossils
are of
footprints
or animal
burrows,
rather than
the animals
themselves.

Petrified fossils are fossils where the bone and other living material have been replaced by deposited minerals.

Most dinosaur
fossils are
actually
petrified
fossils.

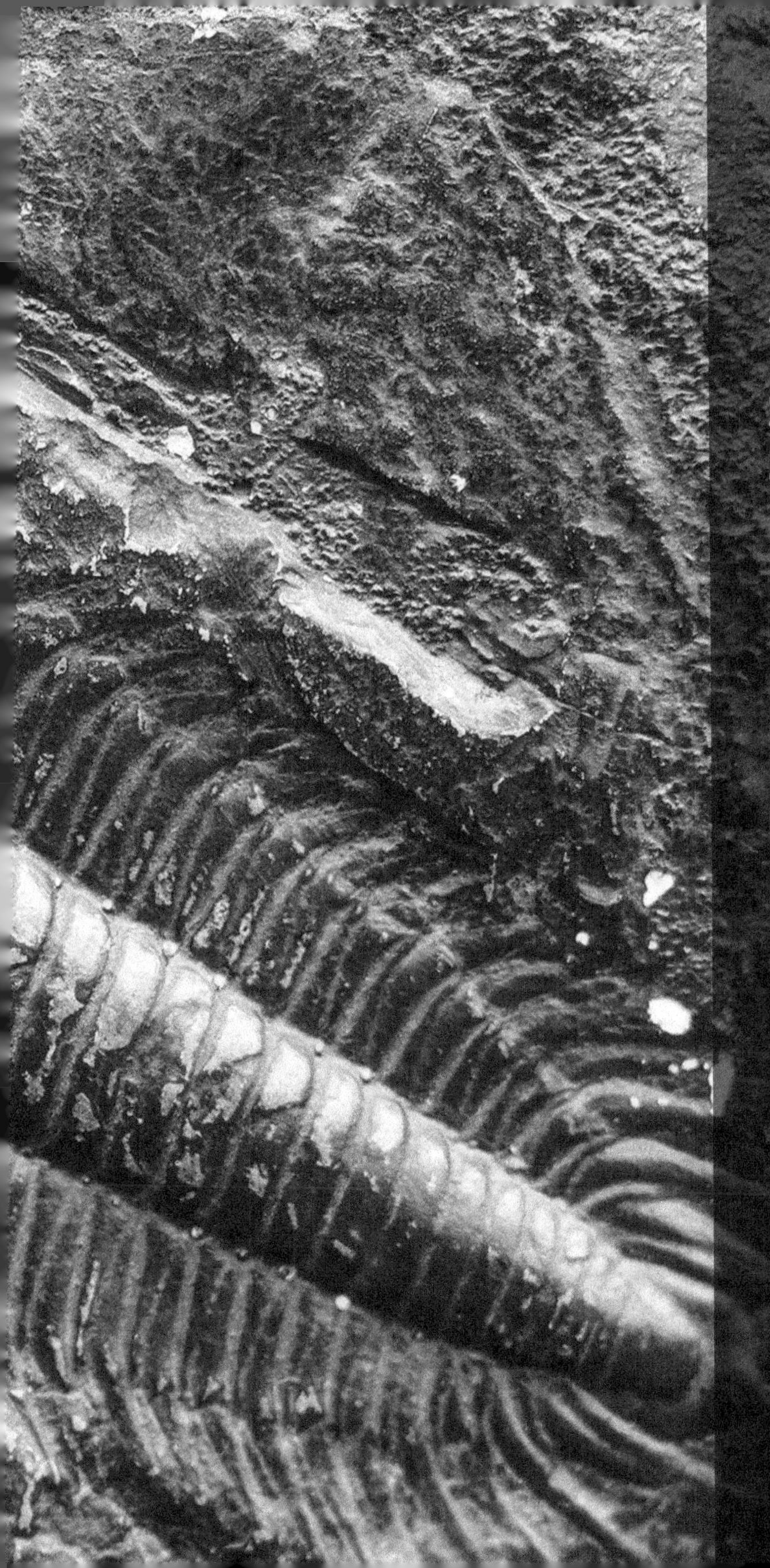

A preserved specimen is called a "fossil" if it is older than some minimum age, most often the arbitrary date of 10,000 years.

Fossils
are found
on every
continent on
Earth including
Antarctica.

Paleontology
is the study
of the history
of life.

It also examines evolution, and how beings have progressed and adapted over time.

Scientists
who study
paleontology
are called
paleontologists.

Paleontologists carefully remove fossils from the ground and record all the details about where and how the fossils were found.

There
are many
different
types of
paleontologists.

Some study fossil plants, some study fossil fish, some study fossil mammals, and some study dinosaurs.

The study of paleontology gives us very important insight into the world, how it was formed, and how animals and plants have evolved.